OF WITCHES AND MONSTERS AND WONDROUS CREATURES

LISL·WEIL

Atheneum   1985   New York

Library of Congress Cataloging in Publication Data
Weil, Lisl.
Of wicked monsters and wondrous creatures.

SUMMARY: Discusses the magical creatures of various cultures since ancient times, such as phoenix, sphinx, dragons, trolls, and witches.
1. Animals, Mythical—Juvenile literature. 2. Monsters—Juvenile literature. [1. Animals, Mythical. 2. Monsters. 3. Folklore] I. Title.
GR825.W4   1985   398.2′454   85-7468
ISBN 0-689-31182-6

Text and pictures copyright © 1985 by Lisl Weil
All rights reserved
Published simultaneously in Canada by
Collier Macmillan Canada, Inc.
Text set by Linoprint Composition, New York City
Printed and bound by the Worzalla Publishing Company,
Stevens Point, Wisconsin
Designed by Mina Greenstein
First Edition

Of Witches, Monsters and Wondrous Creatures

Things are always happening that no one can explain. Today, we look for the answers in science. But long ago people did not have science. And they decided that magical creatures often held the answers. Some of these creatures were good; some were bad. Some were like animals; some were like people. But whatever they were like, they lived everywhere, and because they had magical powers, people had to pay attention to them.

In the beginning, most such creatures were animals. People have always admired some of the things animals are or can do. It would be nice to be strong as a bull or swift as a gazelle. And it would be fun to swim like a seal or fly like a robin. So people thought of animals that were even more powerful than real animals. And they thought of humanlike creatures who had the abilities of animals. Some of these became gods; and some became creatures who simply existed to help or to make life unpleasant for people.

This happened all around the world. Every country, every different group of people, had their own wicked monsters and wondrous creatures that became a part of the stories that were told and the ideas that were believed. Statues were made of these creatures, poems written about them, music composed to celebrate their powers. Some of these beings are long forgotten, but others we still find in statue, story and song. We no longer believe in their magical powers, but we still enjoy hearing and thinking about them. Maybe because secretly we hope that there is a bit of magic in the world.

   The ancient Egyptians believed that there were many magical animals: the ram, the bull, birds, monkeys, snakes, cats and dogs. If they liked you, they could help you; if they didn't like you, they could see that bad things happened to you. Cats, especially, were considered to be so important that killing one was punished by death.
   But not all odd creatures bothered with everyday events in the lives of people. In very early times in Egypt, the symbol for the king was the lion, because the lion was so strong. A great statue was built with a lion body and the head of the pharoah, the king. A creature with a lion's body and another kind of head is called a sphinx. This sphinx was 240 feet long and 66 feet high. It can still be seen, even though it is now over four thousand five hundred years old. When people in Egypt no longer remembered that it had been built to honor a king, it became the symbol of their sun god, Ra.

    Another symbol of the sun god Ra was the phoenix. This was a bird that represented eternal life to the Egyptians. It lived for at least five hundred years. Then, at the proper time, it would build itself a pile of dry branches and leaves and settle down upon them. Facing toward the sun, and waving its wings, it would set the branches and leaves on fire. The hot flames soon burned the phoenix to ashes. But nine days later, out of the ashes came another and more beautiful phoenix.

    The first job of the new phoenix was to fashion an egg out of the ashes and carry it to the temple of the sun, where the priests would guard it forever.

The Egyptians were not the only ones who created stories and myths and legends about fantastic beings. The Greeks and Romans also had tales to tell. Some of these were about strange and wonderful beasts, some about creatures that were half animal and half human, and some were about mythical beings who were sometimes in human form and sometimes not. The chief of the gods (Zeus for the Greeks and Jupiter for the Romans) liked to wander around the earth in the form of an animal, often a bull. People who met animals that did odd things could not be sure if it was a real animal or a god.

The Greeks also had a legend about a different kind of bull, very fierce and powerful, called the Minotaur. This bull was kept by King Minos of Crete in a labyrinth, an area of endless passages and chambers, like a maze. The Minotaur fed on human flesh. Every year seven youths and seven maidens were sent into the labyrinth and never seen again.

One year a handsome prince named Theseus was one of the seven youths to be devoured by the Minotaur. But Theseus and Ariadne, daughter of King Minos, had fallen in love. So Ariadne gave Theseus a ball of string to unwind as he went into the labyrinth. Theseus killed the Minotaur with his sword and escaped the labyrinth by following the string back out.

Theseus and Ariadne sailed away to start a new life together. But as they stopped to rest on the island of Naxos, a goddess appeared and sent Theseus off to do another great deed. Ariadne was left behind. She was not alone for long, however. A god named Bacchus, also sometimes called Dionysius, came to comfort her.

Cerberus was a different kind of Greek monster. He lived along the river Styx, which divided the world of the living from the world of the dead. It was his job to keep the dead in place, but also to keep the living from bothering them. He had three heads and the tail of a snake. Yet it was said that three honey cakes would tame him completely. It may have been with honey cakes that the hero Hercules managed to capture Cerberus.

The Greeks also had sphinxes. One of them had the head of a woman and also had wings. She was very clever about thinking up riddles. Sitting beside a road, she would shout a riddle at passersby, and if they could not answer, she would eat them. The sphinx got quite fat.

One day she posed her riddle to a young prince named Oedipus.

"What moves on four legs in the morning, on two legs at noon, and on three legs in the evening?"

Oedipus thought a moment and then said, "Man as an infant crawls on four legs, morning; as an adult he walks on two legs, noon; and as an old person uses a cane, evening."

The sphinx was so angry at hearing the correct answer that she blew herself into a million pieces.

More helpful than the sphinx was the wonderful, winged horse named Pegasus. He made it possible for the hero Bellerophon to defeat a dreadful monster. And later, Pegasus created a spring of water simply by putting his feet upon the earth.

Those who drank at the spring Pegasus had created became poets and writers. They were carried into the realm of wonder and fancy by the spirit of the great horse himself. To honor Pegasus, the gods set him in the sky, where he can still be seen as a pattern of stars.

For the Greeks, there were magical creatures everywhere. Nymphs, for example, who were all female, seemed to inhabit all sorts of places. And there were many different kinds. Dryads lived in the forests and trees; Oreads lived in the mountains and in caves; Limoniades watched over meadows and flowers. Naiads could be found in all fresh water, including rivers and streams and fountains. Nereids lived at the bottom of the sea. And some even became stars—the Pleiades. They were all lovely, lighthearted, and enjoyed dancing. But they were not always friendly to people.

Quite different was Pan and his helpers, the fauns. Pan, who played the pipes, had the head of a man—except for his horns and long ears—and the legs of a goat. With his pipes he could charm nymphs and gods alike. He was helpful to shepherds and huntsmen, but often he and his fauns played tricks on lonely travelers in the woods.

Among the nymphs who were not very helpful to people were the Sirens. They could sing beautifully and lived on cliffs near the sea. When ships came by, the lovely voices of the Sirens would lure the sailors to destruction on the rocks. Sirens at first were pictured as having the wings and legs of birds, but the upper bodies and heads of women.

When the great Greek hero, Odysseus, longed to hear the song of the Sirens, he had himself bound to the mast of his ship so he could not steer the ship toward the rocks. And he stopped the ears of his shipmates with wax so they could not hear the fatal sounds.

Belief in Sirens continued long after the ancient Greeks and Romans were gone. Even Christopher Columbus recorded a sighting of Sirens.

In later years, other female creatures came to dwell in the waters of the world, at least in the minds of sailors.

In Germany, the Lorelei, lovely maidens whose bodies ended in fish tails, sat upon rocks above the river Rhine. They, like the Sirens, lured unwary boatmen to their doom on the rocks. The composer Richard Wagner put three Lorelei, or mermaids as they are sometimes called, into his opera *Das Rheingold*.

In France, a similar creature, called Undine, longed for legs so she could dance and for the chance to fall in love with a human man. Her wish was granted. She left the water, took on human form and got married. But one day a week she had to become a mermaid again. She made her husband promise never to look for her on the day she was gone. Unfortunately, one day he did; when he saw her as a mermaid, poor Undine had to return to the sea forevermore.

Some creatures are a part of the legends of every land. The idea of the unicorn seems to have begun in India. It spread to China and then to Europe. There, a favorite unicorn legend was woven into a very famous series of exquisite tapestries.

The unicorn looked like a white horse, except that it had a single horn coming from its forehead. This horn was magical. If it were dipped into a pool of muddy water, the water would become clear. The person who drank out of a unicorn horn would have good health all his life.

Catching a unicorn was difficult. They were fast, fierce and shy. Yet they were gentle, too. They never stepped on a smaller being. And they could always be lured to a maiden of pure spirit. Unfortunately, they were sometimes too trusting. The maidens they approached were not always as pure as they seemed. Some turned the unicorns they caught over to the hunters to be killed for the magic horn.

Dragons, too, have appeared everywhere in the world, at some time or another. At least that is what stories and legends would have us believe.

The Greek hero Hercules slew a dragon that never slept and guarded a hoard of golden apples.

The dragons of China and the Far East were rather kind and wise. Emperors looked to them for advice. And they could generally be counted on to be helpful. Such dragons were said to live in a gold and coral palace.

In olden times in Europe there were two kinds of dragons, those with wings and those without. Neither kind seemed wise or helpful, generally. They tended to steal and imprison princesses and guard treasures. Brave knights who tried to free a princess or win a treasure had to face the fiery breath of the dragon and the whip of its powerful tail, to say nothing of encountering its great teeth and its sharp claws. Such dragons appear in many tales, mostly from the Middle Ages.

When the people of China needed rain, they made a huge dragon out of paper and wood and carried it about in the streets. If it did not rain, they destroyed the dragon. And such paper dragons are still used in Chinese ceremonies. They look colorful and mysterious, winding down the street, and everyone enjoys seeing them.

To this day, also, in the city of Tarascon in France, a dragon figure is paraded on a special day. This dragon is helpful because it is supposed to keep the river Rhone from flooding.

Not a dragon, but as strange and as fierce, was the odd creature called Baba Yaga by the Russians. She was an ugly old woman with a very long nose, long teeth and uncombed hair. She rode through the air in a magic bowl, always carrying her magic broom. But strangest of all was her house. It had a large clock on one side and stood on chicken legs. When Baba Yaga wanted to get in, she could fly in, in her magic bowl, or she could say the magic words and the house would stoop down to let her walk in the door.

Baba Yaga liked to eat people. She sailed around in her bowl trying to capture her next meal.

A very different sort of creature, also appearing in Russian folk tales, was the firebird. One of the firebird stories was put to music by Stravinsky and is danced as a ballet.

In this story Prince Ivan catches a firebird. The bird struggles, but the prince holds it tight. Finally, the bird promises the prince a feather that will save his life if he will let go. The prince, by this time, feels sorry for the bird and does let it go. In return he receives the feather.

A few minutes later the prince sees twelve beautiful maidens, followed by a still lovelier young woman, who looks very sad. She is a princess. Prince Ivan falls in love with her on sight. And the princess loves the prince.

The princess begs Prince Ivan to leave at once. She is under the spell of a dreadful magician—a wicked monster who allows her and her maidens to appear only rarely as themselves. The rest of the time they are monsters, too. If the prince does not want to be captured, he must leave.

But Prince Ivan does not leave. He stays and is captured by the monster. At first the prince does not know what to do. But then he remembers the firebird. He touches the feather.

The minute Prince Ivan puts his finger on the feather, the

firebird is there beside him. The monster and his helpers are frozen with fear. Quickly the firebird shows Prince Igor a magic box in a tree. Inside the box is an egg. When that egg is destroyed, the monster, too, will be destroyed. Prince Igor loses no time in breaking the egg. With that, the monster is gone, the princess and her ladies are restored to their rightful shapes, and so are many other young men and women. The prince and the princess are married, of course. And the firebird goes smiling on its way.

Not all monsters and wondrous creatures are huge, or even the size of human beings. Some can be tiny.

The people of Ireland tell about leprechauns, who are very tiny old men. They like to play tricks on people. Leprechauns are said to be keepers of crocks of gold, buried at secret spots. If a person can catch a leprechaun and hold onto him, the leprechaun must tell where there is a pot of gold. But very few people have ever seen a leprechaun, and all those who have have been tricked out of the gold by the cunning creature they caught.

In Germany, tales are told of similar beings called *Heinzelmannchen.* They are helpful little men who may finish and polish the boots the shoemaker has not had time to complete. Or perhaps they will sew up and press the pants the tailor had not quite finished.

Like unicorns and dragons, giants are monsters that have appeared in the stories of almost every country. Giants are generally very tall and strong, but they are not always very wise. However, the Scandinavians, the Greeks, and the American Indians all believed that the very first people to live on Earth were giants.

Among the giants the Greeks told about were the Cyclops, gigantic men with a single eye in the middle of the forehead.

One of the oldest pieces of English literature tells the tale of the hero Beowulf. The people around him were being killed by a fierce giant monster named Grendel. But Beowulf was smarter than Grendel, and when the giant came to kill Beowulf and his men, it was Grendel who died. Later, Beowulf also killed Grendel's mother.

Grendel was a very evil creature, not too different from the demons and devils that also appear in many myths and legends. These were often ugly, manlike creatures, sometimes with a tail and animal legs, or even horns. Some African people and some American Indians made masks of such evil creatures in order to frighten away other evil spirits or to make the creatures themselves powerless.

Japanese people, even today, may do something they call "casting out the devil." Dried beans are thrown toward the four corners of the room in order to catch the devil wherever it may be and drive it out.

Witches may be the kind of monster that is best known to people in western Europe and America. People have believed in witches since Roman times or before. They are women and men with certain kinds of supernatural powers—sometimes good, sometimes evil. Bad ones are thought to be in league with a devil. Such witches can make people, or their animals, ill, can fly through the air, or can cast spells on people to make them do things they do not want to do. Good witches can heal people, can help them in trouble and can make life easier for them. Some bad witches appear in Shakespeare's play *Macbeth*.

People in the past believed so firmly in witches that in various periods of history there were witch trials. People suspected of being witches were put to death. The town of Salem, Massachusetts, became famous for its witch trials, held in 1692.

The best known witch in fairy tales may be the witch in "Hansel and Gretel." She lives in a gingerbread house and tries to fatten up Hansel so she can eat him. But instead it is the witch who is cooked in the fire.

Other beings people all over the world know, in one form or another, are fairies. They may or may not have wings. They can be large or small. But whatever they look like, they can grant wishes, and they often help people like Cinderella, who have problems they cannot solve themselves. There are also wicked fairies who behave like the one in Sleeping Beauty, who cast a spell over the princess and made her sleep for a hundred years.

In folk and fairy tales, there are also elves and gnomes and trolls, as well as animals, who are not like the animals of Greece and Egypt, but who are really human beings of a sort, in disguise. Like the wolf in the story of Red Riding Hood, they often trap human beings into dangerous situations.

 Though today most of us do not believe in the creatures we read about in "once upon a time" tales, we remember them and we remember the things they do and say. They help us to understand ourselves and the things we do and say.
 In all of us there is good and bad, and the monsters and wondrous creatures we read about express some of our feelings about things that happen to us. In folk and fairy tales, in legend and myth, good almost always wins over evil, though sometimes not easily. Reading such stories can make us believe that the future may be good for us, too, with or without magic.